TRACK & TRACE
COVID-19

Welcome to the "covid" book. This is where we write what's inside although you probably flicked through before you bought it so this is somewhat redundant but none the less its here.So what will you find in this rip roaring, action packed vessel of pure joy? Well mainly colouring in, activities to solve, rather odd puzzles that you'll probably just skip; pages to cut out that will just make a mess and leave you asking yourself was it worth it?

Sound entertai
Good luck

GW00493483

If you really struggle the answers are in the back

DRAW A HAPPY FACE

TO MAKE COVID SMILE!

NOBODY WANTS CORONA, HE'S FEELING SAD AND LONELY.....LET'S MAKE HIM HAPPY!

SPOT THE

FIND THE 10 DIFFERENCES

DIFFERENCE

BETWEEN THE 2 BORIS'

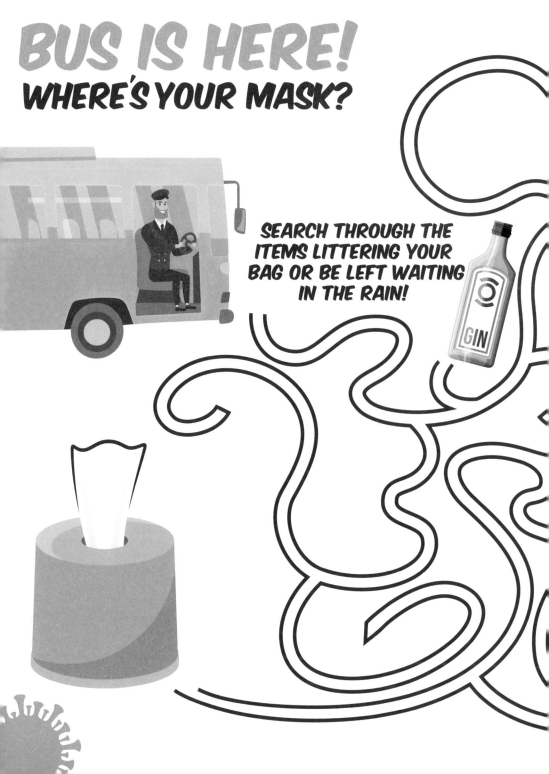

COPY THE LOCKDOWN BOOZE

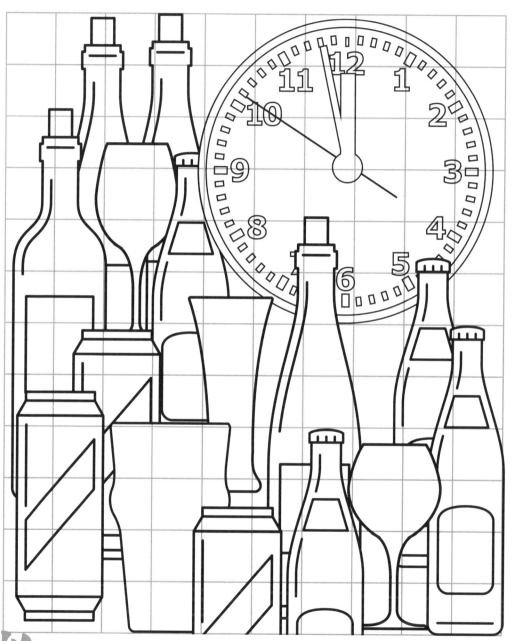

IT'S 12 O'CLOCK SOMEWHERE

THE RULES

(SET THIS WEEKS RESTRICTIONS)

THIS WEEK MASKS DO/DO NOT HELP TO STOP
THE SPREAD

·

SEEING FRIENDS IN THE PUB IS
LEGAL/ILLEGAL /INCENTIVISED

·

I CAN MEET OUTSIDE WITH ___ PEOPLE TODAY

·

THIS WEEK HOLIDAYS ARE LEGAL/ILLEGAL

·

YOU ARE REQUIRED/NOT REQUIRED TO WORK
FROM HOME

THE PRIMARY DIRECTIVE FOR THE CURRENT CLIMATE IS TO KEEP THE ECONOMY TICKING WHILST LETTING SOCIAL AND MENTAL HEALTH TAKE THE
TOLL. WE WILL INTRODUCE SCHEMES TO ENCOURAGE LARGE GROUPS OF PEOPLE TO GATHER AND SPEND. THIS WILL THEN BE A PERFECT
SCAPEGOAT TO BLAME INDIVIDUALS RATHER THAN THE LACK OF EFFECTIVE PLAN PUT IN PLACE BY THIS COUNTRY'S ELITE.

(INCOMPETENCE IN CHARGE)

DESIGN YOUR OWN
ISOLATION DOOR HANGER!

STAY AWAY

COME WITH BOOZE ONLY!

DESIGN YOUR OWN
ISOLATION DOOR HANGER

STAY AWAY

CATS WELCOME

WARNING INFECTIOUS PERSONALITY

DESIGN YOUR MASK

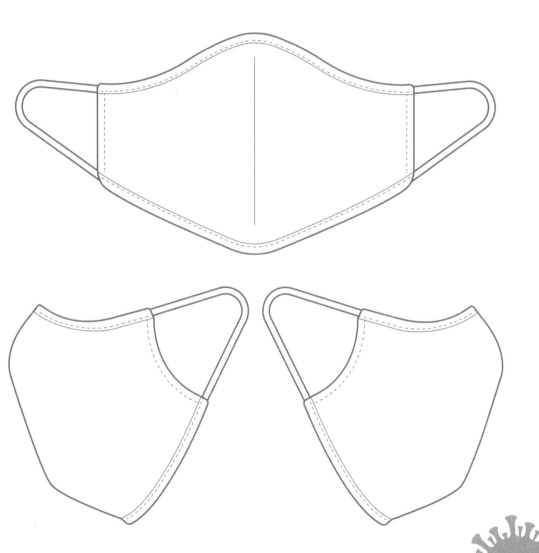

MEET THE NEIGHBOURS YOU NEVER KNEW!

COVID IS MUTATING

SPOT THE

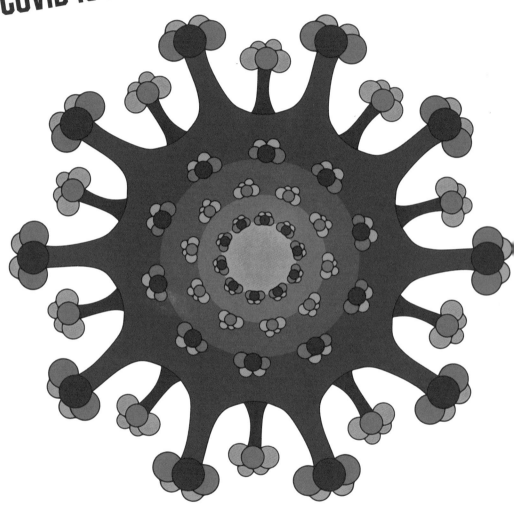

FIND THE 10 DIFFERENCES

DIFFERENCE

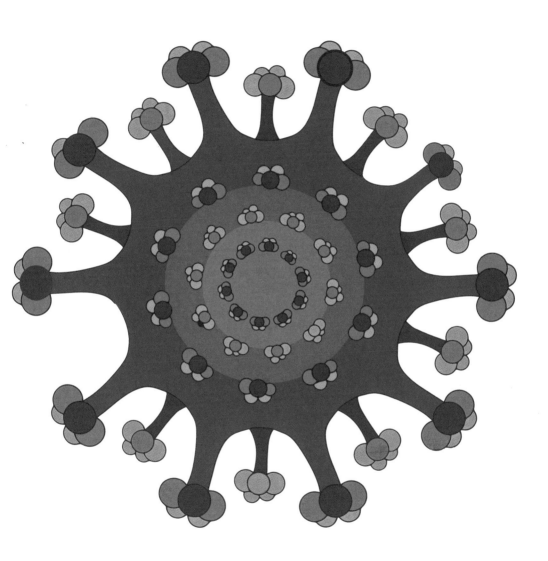

BETWEEN THE 2 COVIDS

POST CORONA OPPORTUNITIES

DRAW YOUR PREDICTIONS OF WHAT HAPPENS NEXT!

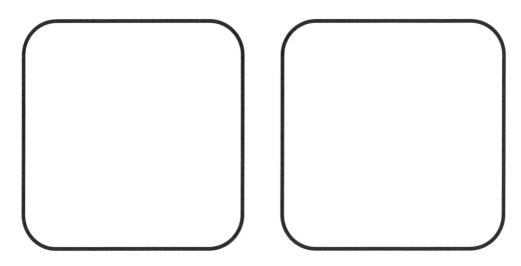

CHOOSE YOUR FAVOURITE:

DINOSAURS RISE AGAIN
ALIENS INVADE
6G IS INVENTED
TRUMP INJECTS BLEACH
LIFE ON VENUS
ROBOTS
PIGS FLYING!
LEO WINS ANOTHER OSCAR

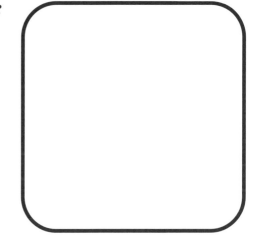

CORONALPHABET

ADD A PANDEMIC RELATED WORD FOR EACH LETTER!

A. _____

B. _____

C. _____

D. _____

E. _____

F. _____

G. _____

H. _____

I. _____

J. _____

K. _____

L. _____

M. _____

N. _____

O. _____

P. _____

Q. _____

R. _____

S. _____

T. _____

U. _____

V. _____

W. _____

X. _____

Y. _____

Z. _____

TRUMP'S SPRING CLEAN REGIME
DRAW THE LIQUID IN THE GLASS AND SYRINGE

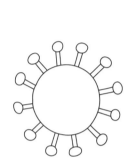

**HOW MUCH
DISINFECTANT
WILL KILL THE VIRUS?**

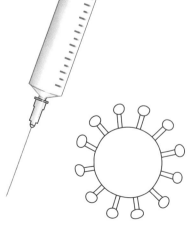

"AND THEN I SEE THE DISINFECTANT WHERE IT KNOCKS IT OUT IN A MINUTE. ONE MINUTE. AND IS THERE A WAY WE CAN DO SOMETHING LIKE THAT, BY INJECTION OR ALMOST A CLEANING?"

"I'M NOT A DOCTOR. BUT I'M, LIKE, A PERSON THAT HAS A GOOD YOU-KNOW-WHAT"

DONALD TRUMP

24TH APRIL 2020

FINISH THE DRAWING

WHAT DOES BORIS' LOCKDOWN HAIR LOOK LIKE TODAY?

URGENT EYETEST!

COPY THE COVID

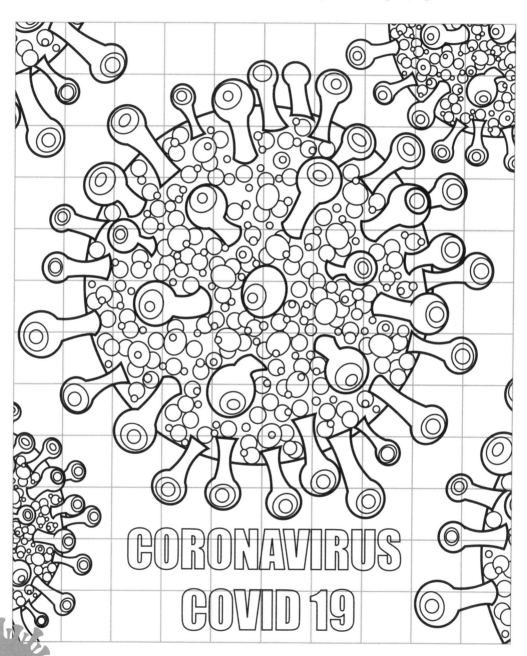

HELP THEM MULTIPY!

GAIN VITAL SUPPLIES!

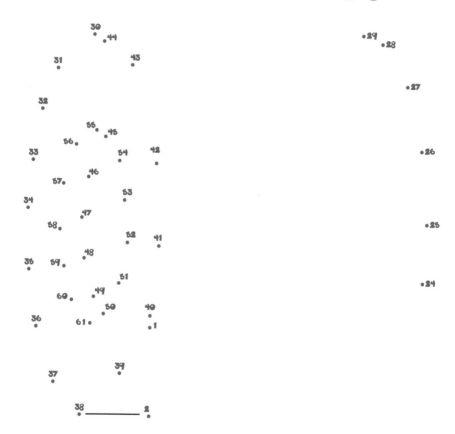

JOIN THE DOTS SO YOU DON'T MISS A SPOT!

COVID CROSSWORD

ACROSS:

1. APPLY WHEN ENTERING SHOPS, (4,9)
2. SHORT SUPPLY EARLY IN THE PANDEMIC, (3)
3. TRUMP'S FAVOURITE HOUSEHOLD ITEM, (6)

DOWN:

1. NOT ONLY FOR HALLOWEEN, (4,4)
2. VERY "HANDY" ITEM, (6)
3. PORTABLE WINDOW, (5)
4. STAY POSITIVE, (4,4)
5. HAPPY BIRTHDAY TO YOU, (4,4)
6. WIPE YOUR WORRIES AWAY, (6)

SOMEONE'S BEEN PANIC BUYING!
RESTOCK THE SHELVES!

£10.99   £4.99   £3.50

£1.99   **BABY WIPES**   £8.70   £2.49

£1.99   **PASTA**   £3.49   £6.49

£3.99   **BOOZE**   £5.99

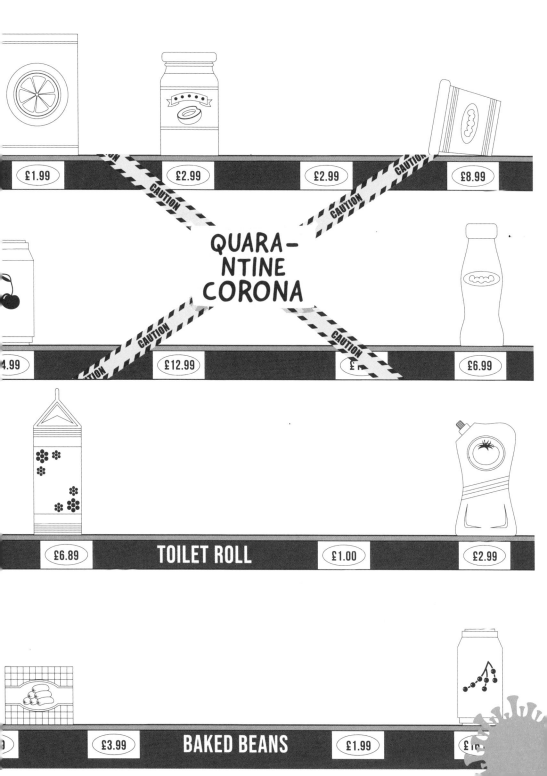

COPY THE LOCKDOWN EXCERCISE ROUTINE

NO LOCKDOWN STONE FOR YOU!

COLOUR ME IN

STAY ALERT ▷ CONTROL THE VIRUS ▷ SAVE LIVES

"I WAS AT THE HOSPITAL THE OTHER NIGHT WHERE I THINK THERE
WERE A FEW CORONAVIRUS PATIENTS AND I SHOOK HANDS WITH
EVERYBODY, YOU WILL BE PLEASED TO KNOW,
AND I CONTINUE TO SHAKE HANDS."

BORIS JOHNSON

3RD MARCH 2020

FLATTEN THE CURVE

TRACK AND TRACE THE 9 ITEMS BELOW:

 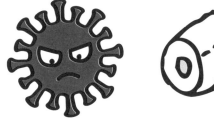 

My Pre-Lockdown Self Portrait

16TH MARCH- BORIS JOHNSON: "NOW IS THE TIME FOR EVERYONE TO STOP NON-ESSENTIAL CONTACT WITH OTHERS AND TO STOP ALL UNNECESSARY TRAVEL"

23RD MARCH- BORIS JOHNSON: "IF YOU DON'T FOLLOW THE RULES THE POLICE WILL HAVE THE POWERS TO ENFORCE THEM, INCLUDING THROUGH FINES"

27TH MARCH- DOMINIC CUMMINGS DRIVES 260 MILES TO DURHAM. GOVERNMENT GUIDELINES STATED: "YOU SHOULD NOT BE VISITING FAMILY MEMBERS WHO DO NOT LIVE IN YOUR HOME."

24TH MAY- BORIS JOHNSON SAYS MR CUMMINGS "ACTED RESPONSIBLY, LEGALLY AND WITH INTEGRITY"

25TH MAY- DOMINIC CUMMINGS "I DROVE THE THREE OF US UP TO DURHAM LAST NIGHT, ARRIVING ROUGHLY AT MIDNIGHT."
"NO, I DON'T REGRET WHAT I DID."

COLOUR ME IN

CUT + STICK GUIDANCE

CREATE YOUR OWN GOVERMENT MESSAGE

USE PUBLIC TRANSPORT	DON'T USE PUBLIC TRANSPORT
GO ON HOLIDAY	DON'T GO ON HOLIDAY
WORK FROM HOME	GO TO WORK
WEAR A MASK	DON'T WEAR A MASK

EXTRA ADVICE ON THE BACK!

ADVISE THE NATION

SAVE LIVES	CONTROL THE VIRUS
STAY HOME	STAY ALERT
EAT OUT TO HELP OUT	PROTECT THE NHS
WASH YOUR HANDS	SOCIAL DISTANCE

STAYCATION

WHICH COUNTRIES ARE QUARANTINED THIS WEEK?

A	Z	U	X	D	M	J	E	S	X	X	H	⊙	C	F
V	S	R	W	F	A	P	A	C	K	L	I	⊙	U	U
F	N	D	Z	C	V	S	E	A	A	X	T	Y	A	X
Q	L	E	D	B	⊙	S	D	M	K	Y	A	N	S	E
D	N	A	L	A	E	Z	W	E	N	G	L	A	N	D
U	N	I	G	L	F	L	Y	R	N	D	Y	M	Y	V
U	V	Z	A	U	T	K	I	I	S	C	T	R	B	E
Z	M	W	V	P	T	H	S	C	R	Q	Z	E	I	K
H	W	N	N	G	S	R	C	A	⊙	Z	I	G	S	D
U	V	S	P	E	P	B	⊙	W	P	N	V	E	M	A
Y	S	H	K	N	D	V	T	P	D	V	⊙	M	R	Z
E	N	I	A	K	B	E	L	I	G	M	N	U	P	E
T	L	U	J	D	D	N	A	L	E	R	I	V	I	Z
W	C	G	E	P	E	A	N	I	H	C	L	R	F	F
Z	K	Y	I	A	M	Q	D	T	M	F	L	Y	N	M

AMERICA   CHINA   ENGLAND
GERMANY   INDIA   IRELAND
ITALY   NEW ZEALAND   PORTUGAL
SCOTLAND   SPAIN   WALES

COLOUR ME IN

COVID-19 HOSPITALIS

60 000
55 000
50 000
45 000
40 000
35 000
30 000
25 000
20 000
15 000
10 000
5 000
0

17   20   04   19   22   01   10
Mar   Mar   Apr   Apr   Apr   May   M

IN THE US

" WE PRETTY MUCH SHUT IT DOWN COMING IN FROM CHINA.
IT'S GOING TO BE FINE"

DONALD TRUMP
2ND FEBRUARY 2020

"WE DO NOT RECOMMEND FACE MASKS FOR GENERAL WEARING BY THE PUBLIC"

PROFESSOR JONATHAN VAN-TAM
DEPUTY CHIEF MEDICAL OFFICER
3RD APRIL 2020

"YES, FACE COVERINGS, I THINK PEOPLE SHOULD BE WEARING THEM IN SHOPS"

BORIS JOHNSON

13TH JULY 2020

MAKE A VACCINE
CUT AND STICK TO MAKE YOUR COVID CURE

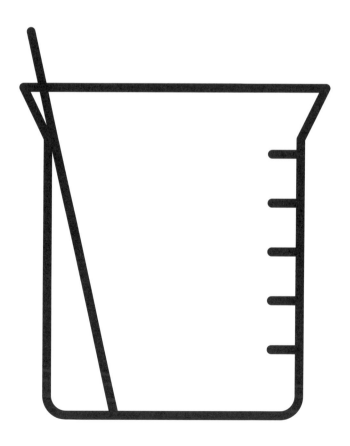

INGREDIENTS
WHICH ITEMS WILL YOU CHOOSE?

TRACK THE WORDS

Y	Y	Q	J	W	P	J	I	S	A	L	K	K	A	S
S	C	U	B	A	T	V	G	Z	I	L	⚙	J	W	J
S	I	A	G	K	G	S	Q	I	⚙	⚙	B	E	N	Y
C	P	R	R	J	Z	K	Q	U	M	R	W	N	U	X
N	E	J	⚙	I	T	R	U	M	P	T	Z	J	P	H
U	P	K	⚙	B	P	Y	W	R	Y	E	P	Z	X	N
H	X	T	N	X	Q	S	Q	I	M	L	D	X	L	N
T	C	⚙	R	⚙	N	A	N	Q	⚙	I	G	J	W	C
Y	⚙	V	Y	A	V	R	G	⚙	L	⚙	K	⚙	Q	H
M	M	M	G	I	V	L	K	L	C	T	D	E	M	I
G	F	F	R	I	Z	E	⚙	T	I	K	B	N	P	N
Y	F	U	S	⚙	⚙	Z	L	S	C	K	A	X	Y	A
Z	S	M	K	D	J	S	X	⚙	S	K	W	Q	W	V
X	R	L	I	R	S	S	L	A	Q	S	S	X	J	J
R	U	S	M	H	J	X	M	E	N	C	S	E	R	I

BAT	CORONA	TOILETROLL
BORIS	LOCKDOWN	TRAVEL
CHINA	MASK	TRUMP
CONSPIRACY	SWAB	VIRUS

DOTTY DONALD

JOIN THE DOTS, REVEAL A DONALD!

" IF WE TESTED LESS, THERE WOULD BE LESS CASES"

DONALD TRUMP
1ST AUGUST 2020

PANDEMIC PASTIMES

TRACK DOWN YOUR LOCKDOWN APPROVED ACTIVITIES

Y	S	Z	L	J	T	P	U	W	Y	C	H	T	K	S
P	U	P	P	Y	P	I	C	T	U	R	E	S	P	K
Z	S	Q	R	T	I	G	E	R	K	I	N	G	I	D
N	M	V	Q	I	U	C	D	R	I	N	K	I	N	G
E	B	V	A	✹	N	C	Y	I	D	L	P	E	M	W
W	A	L	K	I	N	G	R	C	X	I	W	V	A	Y
D	K	K	N	I	T	D	C	I	L	L	I	T	E	T
I	I	✹	A	I	D	E	M	L	A	I	C	✹	S	I
E	N	✹	G	C	C	H	✹	N	E	H	N	B	I	P
T	G	B	✹	R	C	W	G	I	T	A	F	G	C	F
H	H	S	Y	T	F	U	N	V	P	C	N	L	R	L
N	R	I	U	✹	A	M	E	D	I	T	A	T	E	E
W	N	H	R	G	N	I	P	E	E	L	S	K	X	S
G	T	T	E	L	F	✹	C	X	I	L	F	T	E	N
H	S	Y	R	T	E	✹	P	J	F	U	N	Z	T	N

24 TO FIND

LOCKDOWN BINGO.

PLAY WITH A FRIEND CUT THE CARDS OUT AND KEEP TRACK OF YOUR COVID JOURNEY.

ATE OUT TO HELP OUT	FORGOT YOUR MASK AT THE SHOP	APPLIED TOO MUCH SANITISER
COUGHED IN PUBLIC	FREE SQUARE	BEEN ON FURLOUGH
STEPPED INTO TRAFFIC TO AVOID PEOPLE	CUT YOUR OWN HAIR	CANCELLED PLANS TO AVOID CORONA

COMPLAINED ABOUT THE GOVERNMENT	HAD A RANT ON SOCIAL MEDIA	REUSED A DISPOSABLE MASK
GONE THE WRONG WAY IN A ONE WAY SYSTEM	FREE SQUARE	BROKE THE RULES MEETING OTHERS
GIVEN FALSE TRACK AND TRACE INFO	GRASSED ON NEIGHBOURS FOR SEEING FAMILY	BROKE A RULE YOU DIDN'T KNOW ABOUT

CLOSER THAN 2M BETWEEN SOMEONE IN THE QUEUE	HAD MORE THAN 2 TAKEAWAYS THIS WEEK	HAD A PANDEMIC GARDEN PARTY
AVOIDED SQUIRTING SANITISER AT THE DOOR	FREE SQUARE	PANIC BOUGHT ITEMS YOU REALLY DIDN'T NEED
LAUGHED AT SOMEBODY'S DIY MASK	REUSED A DISPOSABLE MASK	ATE OUT TO HELP OUT

TRACK & TRACE THE VIRUS

THIS COVID PAIR

ONLY APPEAR TOGETHER
ONCE
ON THE OPPOSITE PAGE.
CAN YOU FIND THEM?

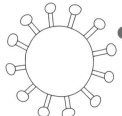

2M DISTANCE! I DON'T WANT:

☐ CORONA

☐ MORE WORK

☐ HUMAN CONTACT

DRAW THE SYMPTOMS

BARNARD CASTLE

"WE AGREED THAT WE SHOULD GO FOR A SHORT DRIVE TO SEE IF I COULD DRIVE SAFELY, WE DROVE FOR ROUGHLY HALF AN HOUR AND ENDED UP ON THE OUTSKIRTS OF BARNARD CASTLE TOWN. WE DID NOT VISIT THE CASTLE, WE DID NOT WALK AROUND THE TOWN.."

DOMINIC CUMMINGS
25TH MAY 2020

COLOUR
ME IN

FIND A TEST CENTRE!

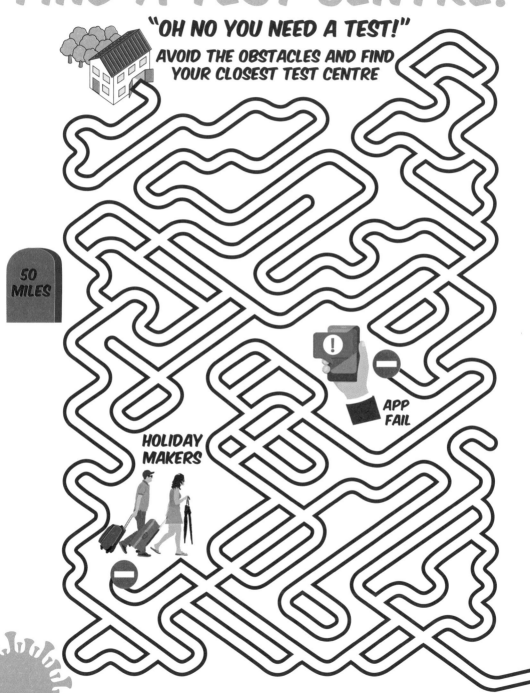

DRAW THE DANGER:

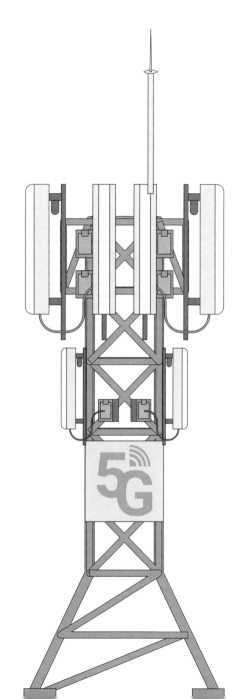

FINISH THE DRAWING
WHAT DOES TRUMP'S LOCKDOWN HAIR LOOK LIKE TODAY?

LOCKDOWN EXERCISES

KEEP YOUR DISTANCE

REACH FOR BISCUITS

OPEN DOOR WITH LEG

GET OFF THE COUCH

AVOID THE COUGH

SHOP OUT OF TOILET ROL

AGRANAMS

CORN SAVIOUR ....

CAMPED IN ....

COLD WONK ....

AHEM TOASTY ....

LION OSTIA ....

ANTIQUE RAN ....

FAKE SCAMS ....

HOBOS JOIN RNS ....

CATINA DISCLOSING ....

SWAB DECIPHER

SOLVE THE ANAGRAMS TO FIGURE OUT WHICH STARS' GOT THE RO

- HAMS KNOT .... _____

- KNIP .... _____

- ABSORPTION TRENT _____

- ANUBIS LOT .... _____

- ANNA DOM .... _____

- ARCHERS PENCIL ..... _____

- JOSH ROBINSON ...... _____

- GROWL JINK .... _____

- KENYA STEW .... _____

- HONEYS JON WAND .... _____

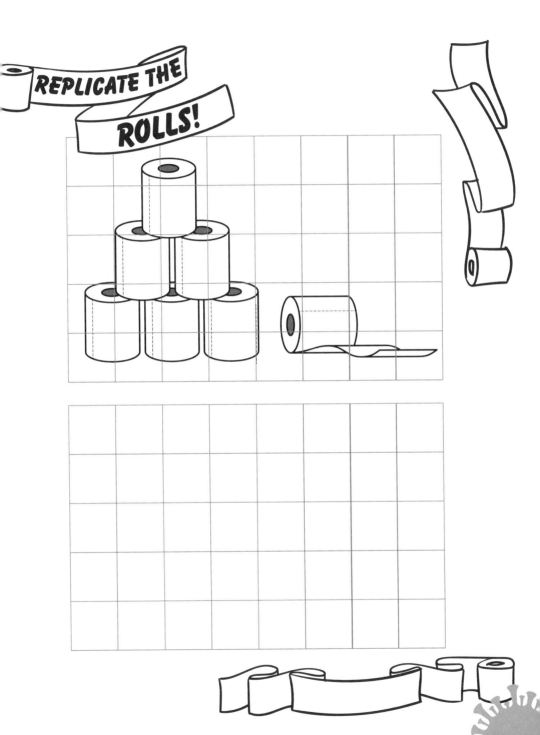

REPLICATE THE ROLLS!

UNCOVER THE
GOVERNMENT
U-TURNS

R	T	S	A	Z	V	X	H	Y	C	M	I	L	H	P
H	E	R	D	I	M	M	U	N	I	T	Y	A	V	C
W	Q	T	A	U	Z	V	A	J	P	D	✹	K	U	N
✹	S	N	U	C	N	E	W	P	V	G	G	W	Q	C
R	C	V	A	R	K	Z	E	A	K	N	Z	C	M	A
K	H	A	F	B	N	A	I	M	I	I	L	A	S	R
F	✹	T	L	K	N	T	N	T	A	T	N	E	C	E
R	✹	G	Y	R	N	✹	✹	D	L	S	I	B	C	H
✹	L	U	H	L	H	V	I	S	T	E	M	M	A	✹
M	M	I	N	K	E	K	D	T	C	T	N	N	E	M
H	E	A	L	T	H	S	U	R	C	H	A	R	G	E
✹	A	L	✹	C	K	D	✹	W	N	I	✹	C	T	S
M	L	M	X	S	R	U	U	N	W	M	V	✹	E	E
E	E	C	A	F	E	X	V	S	L	E	V	E	L	A
R	D	M	Q	R	C	✹	X	Q	G	J	P	E	Z	N

A LEVELS	CARE HOMES	EVICTION BAN
FACE	GCSE	HEALTH SURCHARGE
HERD IMMUNITY	HUAWEI	LOCKDOWN
MASKS	PPE	REMOTE VOTING
TESTING	SCHOOL MEAL	RETURN TO SCHOOL
TRACK AND TRACE		WORK FROM HOME

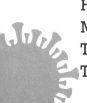

DRAW THE BOGEYS ON THE COVID SWAB

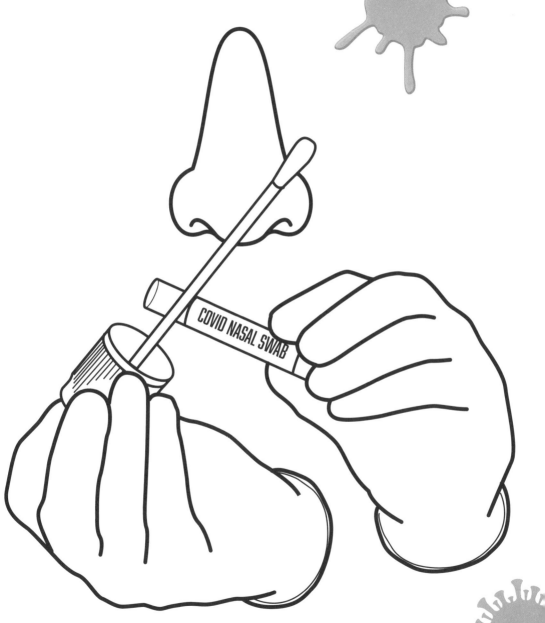

COPY THE PPE ESSENTIALS

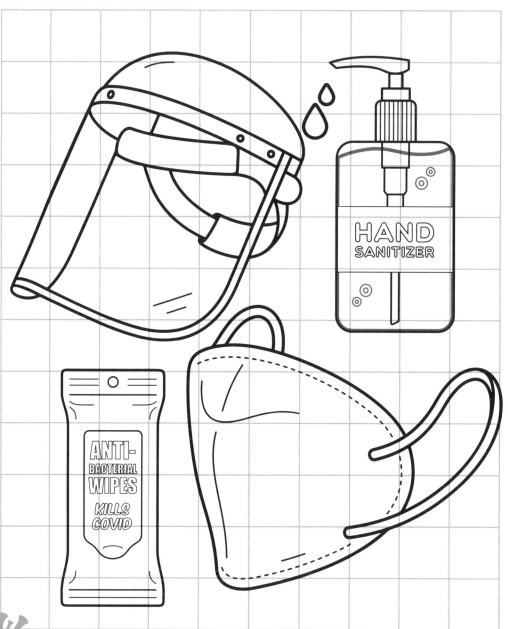

STOCKPILE THE PPE!

MY PET CORONA

My name is .... I am .... days old.
I was adopted on ....
My owner is .... My R rate is ....

My favourite hobby is shopping/visiting pubs/going to
the beach/catching the bus. (delete as applicable)

GIVE ME A FACE
AND COLOUR ME IN

MASK ETIQUETTE
DRAW THE CORRECT METHOD

"TODAY I WANTED TO OUTLINE THE NEXT STEP: A NEW NHS APP FOR CONTACT TRACING. WE'RE ALREADY TESTING THIS APP AND AS WE DO THIS WE'RE WORKING CLOSELY WITH THE WORLD'S LEADING TECH COMPANIES AND RENOWNED EXPERTS IN DIGITAL SAFETY AND ETHICS."

MATT HANCOCK
12TH APRIL 2020

"WE HAVE GROWING CONFIDENCE THAT WE WILL HAVE A TEST, TRACK AND TRACE OPERATION THAT WILL BE WORLD-BEATING AND YES IT WILL BE IN PLACE BY JUNE 1,"

BORIS JOHNSON TOLD PARLIAMENT
20TH MAY 2020

APP DITCHED AFTER FAILING TO WORK.
18TH JUNE 2020

STAY SAFE ▶ TRAP THE VIRUS

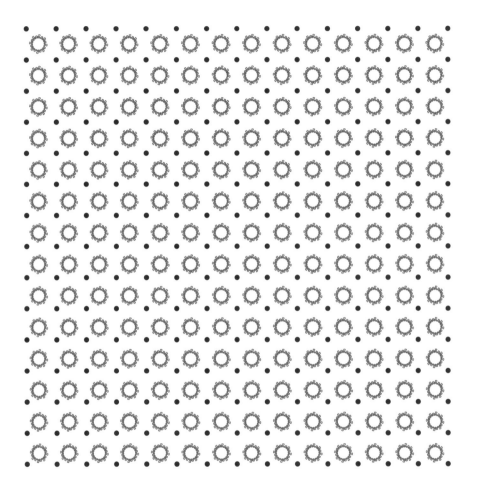

EACH PLAYER TAKES A TURN TO DRAW A LINE FROM DOT TO DOT IN A BID TO FULLY ENLOSE
A COVID IN A BOX- MARK THE TRAPPED COVID WITH PLAYERS COLOUR
THE WINNER IS THE PLAYER WITH THE MOST COVIDS

LOCKDOWN HOBBIES CROSSWORD

ACROSS:

1. LOCKDOWN SPRUCE UP, (6,8)
2. FIX IT UP, (3)
3. WILD AND EXOTIC, (5,4)
4. FROM MANE TO MULLET, (7)

DOWN:

1. WHERE TROLLS HANG OUT, (6,5)
2. TURN ON THE WATERWORKS, (6)
3. TIME TO RHYME, (6)
4. BINGE AND CHILL, (7)
5. THE NEXT NIGELLA, (6)
6. NOT SO THINK AS YOU DRUNK I AM, (8)

COPY THE TESTING SWAB

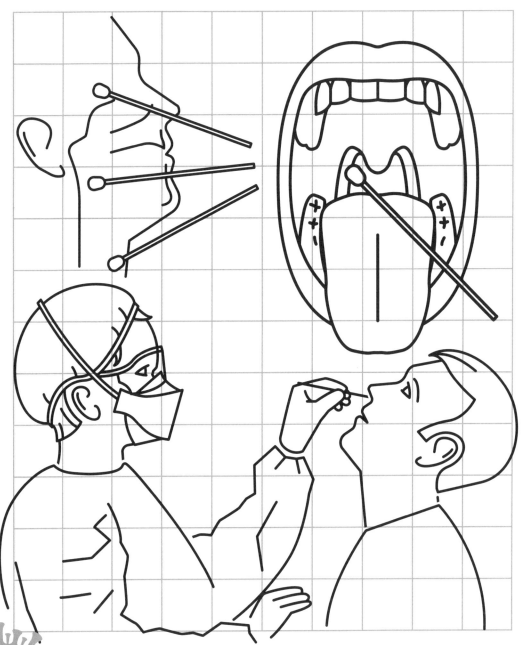

DRIVEN 100 MILES FOR A TEST SWAB?

COVID COMFORTS

MATCH THE COPING MECHANISM TO YOUR FRIENDS AND FAMILY

ANSWERS

GOVERNMENT U-TURNS

R	T	S	A	Z	V	X	H	Y	C	M	I	L	H	P
H	E	R	D	I	M	M	U	N	I	T	Y	A	V	C
W	Q	T	A	U	Z	V	A	J	P	D	O	K	U	N
O	S	N	U	C	N	E	W	V	G	G	W	Q	C	
R	C	V	A	R	K	Z	L	A	K	Z	C	M	A	
I	H	A	F	E	N	A	I	M		L	A	S	R	
F	O	T	L	K	N	T	N	Z	A	T	N	E	C	
R	O	G	Y	R	N	O	D	L	S	I	B	C	H	
O	L	U	H	L	H	V	I	T	E	M	M	A	O	
M	M	I	N	K	L	K	D	T	C	N	N	E	M	
H	E	A	L	T	H	S	U	R	G	E	A	R	O	
O	A	L	O	C	K	D	O	W	N	I	O	C	T	S
M	L	M	X	S	R	U	U	N	W	M	V	O	E	E
L	E	C	A	F	E	X	V	S	L	E	V	E	L	A
K	D	M	Q	R	C	O	X	Q	G	J	P	E	Z	N

PANDEMIC PASTIMES

Y	S	Z	L	J	T	P	U	W	Y	C	H	T	K	S
P	U	P	P	Y	P	I	C	T	U	R	E	S	P	K
Z	S	Q	R	T	I	G	E	R	K	I	N	G	I	D
N	M	V	Q	I	U	G	D	R	I	N	K	I	N	G
E	B	V	A	O	N	G	Y	I	D	L	P	E	M	W
W	A	L	K	I	N	G	P	C	X	W	V	A	Y	
D	K	N	I	T	D	G	I	X	L	I	Z	E	T	
	O	A	I	D	E	M	O	Y	C	O	S			
E	N	O	G	C	C	H	O	N	E	X	N	B		P
T	G	B	O	R	C	W	G	I	T	A	T	G	C	
H	H	S	I	T	T	U	N	V	P	C	N	E	R	L
N	R	U	G	A	M	E	D	I	T	A	T	E		
W	N	H	R	O	N	I	P	E	E	L	S	K	Y	S
G	T	Y	E	L	F	O	C	X	I	L	F	T	E	N
H	S	Y	R	T	E	O	P	J	F	U	N	Z	T	N

TRACK THE WORDS

Y	Y	Q	J	W	P	J	I	S	A	L	K	K	A	S
S	C	U	B	A	T	V	G	Z	I	L	O	J	W	J
S	I	A	G	K	G	S	Q	I	O	O	B	E	N	Y
C	P	R	P	J	Z	K	Q	U	M	R	W	N	U	X
N	E	J	O	I	T	R	U	M	P	T	Z	J	P	H
U	P	K	O	B	P	Y	W	R	Y	E	P	Z	X	N
H	X	T	N	X	Q	S	Q	I	M	L	D	X	L	N
T	G	O	R	O	N	A	N	Q	O		G	J	W	C
Y	O	V	Y	A	V	R	G	O	L	O	K	O	Q	H
M	M	M	G	I	L	K	L	C	T	D	E	M		
G	F	F	R	I	Z	E	O	T	I	K	B	N	P	N
Y	F	L	S	O	O	Z	L	S	C	K	A	X	Y	A
Z	S	M	K	D	J	S	X	O	S	K	W	Q	W	V
X	R	L	I	R	S	S	L	Q	S	S	S	X	J	J
R	U	S	M	H	J	X	M	E	N	C	S	E	R	I

STAYCATION

A	Z	U	X	D	M	J	E	S	X	X	H	O	C	F
V	S	R	W	F	A	P	A	C	K	L	I	O	U	U
F	N	D	Z	C	V	S	E	A	A	X	T	Y	A	X
Q	L	E	D	B	O	S	D	M	K	Y	A	N	S	E
D	N	A	L	A	E	Z	W	I	N	G	A	N	D	
U	N	I	C	L	F	L	Y	R	N	D	Y	M	Y	V
U	V	Z	X	U	T	K	I		S	C	T	R	B	E
Z	M	W	V	R	I	H	S	C	R	Q	Z	E	I	K
H	W	N	N	G	S	P	C	A	O	Z	I	G	S	D
U	V	S	P	E	P	B	W	P	N	V	E	M	A	
Y	S	H	K	N	D	V	I	P	D	V	O	M	R	Z
E	N	I	A	K	B	E	L	I	G	M	N	U	P	E
T	L	U	J	D	E	N	A	L	E	R	I	V	I	Z
W	C	G	E	P	E	A	I	I	H	C	L	R	F	F
Z	K	Y	I	A	M	Q	D	T	M	F	L	Y	N	M

ANSWERS

COVID CROSSWORD

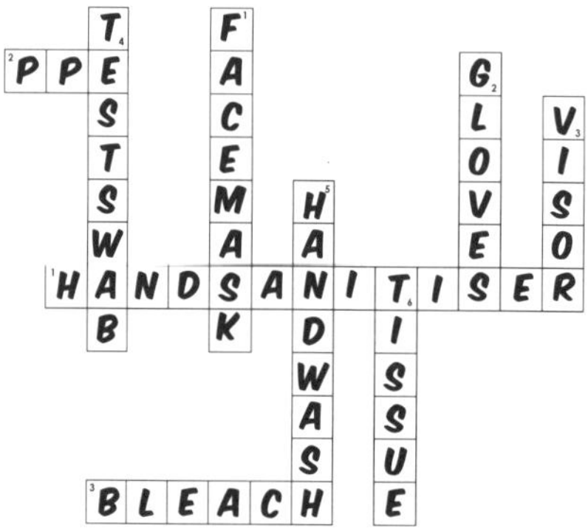

1 HANDSANITISER
2 PPE
3 BLEACH
1 FACEMASK
2 GLOVES
3 VISOR
4 TESTSWAB
5 HANDWASH
6 TISSUE

LOCKWOOD HOBBIES CROSSWORD

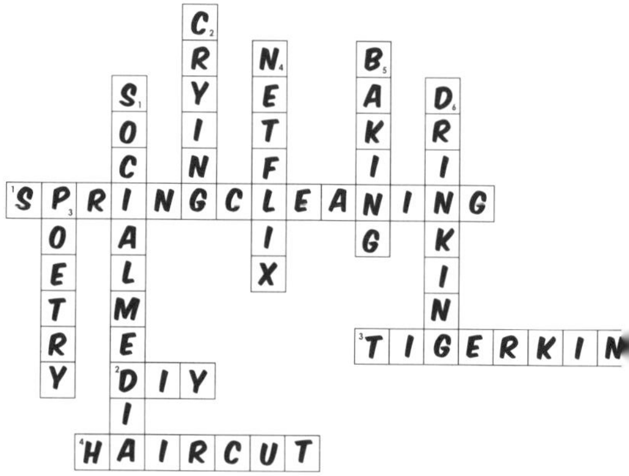

1 SPRINGCLEANING
2 DIY
3 TIGERKIN
4 HAIRCUT
1 SOCIALMEDIA
2 CRYING
3 POETRY
4 NETFLIX
5 BAKING
6 DRINKING

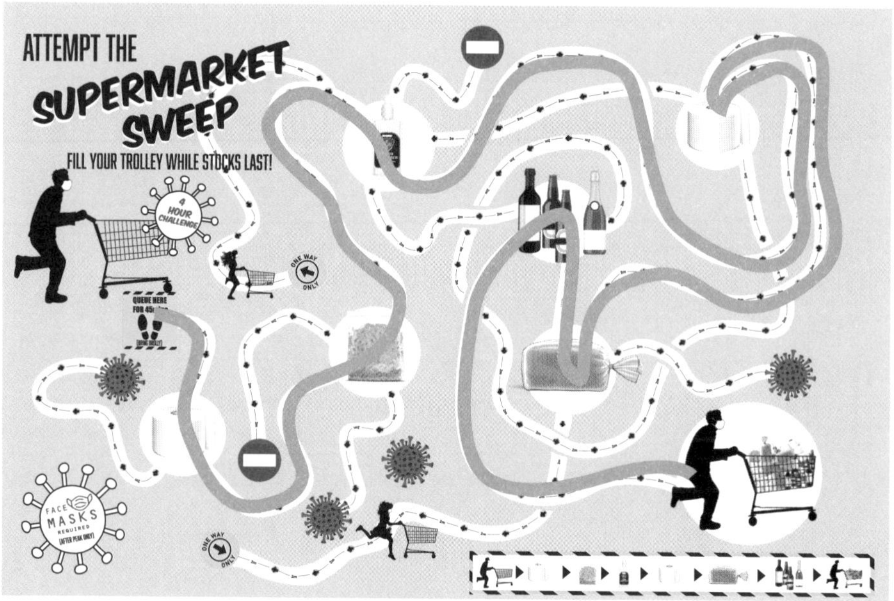

ATTEMPT THE
SUPERMARKET SWEEP
FILL YOUR TROLLEY WHILE STOCKS LAST!
4 HOUR CHALLENGE
ONE WAY ONLY
FACE MASKS REQUIRED (AFTER PEAK ONLY)
ONE WAY ONLY

ANSWERS

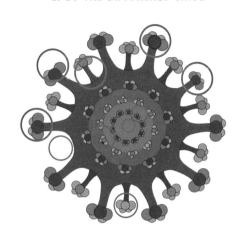

AGRANAMS

CORONAVIRUS
PANDEMIC
LOCKDOWN
STAY AT HOME
ISOLATION
QUARANTINE
FACE MASKS
BORIS JOHNSON
SOCIAL DISTANCING

SWAB DECIPHER

TOM HANKS
PINK
ROBERT PATTINSON
USAIN BOLT
MADONNA
PRINCE CHARLES
BORIS JOHNSON
J.K ROWLING
KANYE WEST
DWAYNE JOHNSON

ANSWERS

FIND A TEST CENTRE!

"OH NO YOU NEED A TEST!"

AVOID THE OBSTACLES FIND YOUR CLOSEST TEST CENTRE

200 MILES AWAY BUT YOU GOT YOUR TEST!

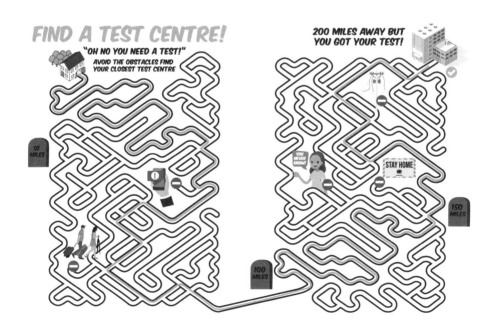

ANSWERS

BUS IS HERE!
WHERE'S YOUR MASK?

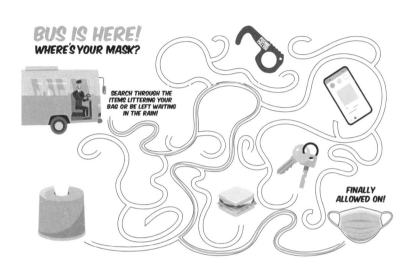

SEARCH THROUGH THE ITEMS LITTERING YOUR BAG OR BE LEFT WAITING IN THE RAIN!

FINALLY ALLOWED ON!

SOD THE RULES!!

BARNARD CASTLE

TRACK & TRACE THE VIRUS!

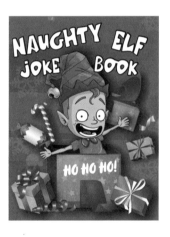